"As exotic as its title, JACK FRUIT MOON is an intriguing document, a lyrical stream of consciousness in the shape of alternating haiku and tanka style poems. It is rich with fantastical language and mysterious images. We can smell the tropics in Wilson's poetry :

> sundown
> the old woman
> scooping
> fish paste
> into recycled bottles

and we can feel the heat of love there :

> dancing with
> lights, your nipples
> lead me to
> the bed we broke last
> night in a haiku

An excitingly different poetic world to read and absorb."
　　—Amelia Fielden, Australian poet and translator.

"The well-known poet and founder of the online literary journal, *Simply Haiku*, Robert Wilson, has written an epoch-making work of vivid tanka-haiku entitled JACK FRUIT MOON. His web haiku, *Vietnam Ruminations*, which I used in my college textbook, *The International-ization of Japanese Poetry*, gave us a strong punch, challenging our lukewarm living. Through JACK FRUIT MOON, he shows us his way of living in the southeast Asian nation, the Philippines, where he lives with his new wife and family. His poetry emotes vivid images of life in the Philippines. When I was younger, I recall the time when my Filipino friend recommended I try 'balut' saying that if I did, I would better understand the Filipino mind and spirit. Enjoy this innovative new tanka and haiku collection. Please taste Robert's cooking in the Philippines!"
　　—Ikuyo Yoshimura, internationally recognized poet, author, speaker, and Associate Professor of English at Asahi University, Gifu, Japan

JACK FRUIT MOON

Jack Fruit Moon

Haiku & Tanka
by
Robert D. Wilson

With a Foreword by Sanford Goldstein
and a Preface by Steven D. Carter

MODERN ENGLISH TANKA PRESS
BALTIMORE, MARYLAND
2009

THE UNEXAMINED LIFE IS NOT WORTH LIVING.

SOCRATES

MODERN ENGLISH TANKA PRESS
P.O. Box 43717, Baltimore, Maryland 21236 USA
www.modernenglishtankapress.com
www.themetpress.com
publisher@modernenglishtankapress.com

Jack Fruit Moon
Copyright 2009 by Robert D. Wilson

Printed in the United States of America

2009

Jack Fruit Moon by Robert D. Wilson

Published by Modern English Tanka Press
Baltimore, Maryland USA

ISBN 978-0-9817691-4-1

publisher@modernenglishtankapress.com
www.modernenglishtankapress.com
www.themetpress.com

Dedication:

This book of poetry is dedicated to:

My wife Jinky, my sons EJ, Carlo, and Levi; my daughters Bobster, Leah, and Krissy, my dear, well-read mother Barbara Wilson, the original liberated woman who was always there for me; and to my father, the late poet and Executive Planning Director for Los Angeles, California, Robert Dean Wilson, who first introduced haiku to me and made it meaningful.

I would also like to acknowledge:

Dana-Maria Onica, Hugh Bygott, Johnye Strickland, Carol Raisfeld, Ikuyo Yoshimura, Amelia Fielden, Kathy Lippard Cobb, Hortensia Anderson, Michael McClintock, Denis Garrison; Professor Steven D. Carter; a dear friend in Virginia who doesn't want to be mentioned; Michael Rehling, Sanford Goldstein, Richard Hastings, Terry Busch, my late sister, Babette Arnuco, my brother, James Richard Wilson, a professor and minister in Botswana, Africa; my sister, Donna Marie Benton; and my late first wife, Ileta Wynell Wilson, who nurtured and encouraged my writing. Without all of you, this book could never have existed. I thank you from the bottom of my heart.

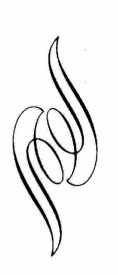

Foreword

In 2008, Robert Wilson asked me to join him in creating a book in which we would alternate our tanka. I had thought I would write a tanka and Robert would respond to it with a tanka of his own. But I became increasingly frustrated, for his tanka did not seem to have anything to do with what I had composed. For example, one of my poems was about a Palestinian film I had recently seen about a Palestinian terrorist who did not want to carry through his mission of killing innocent Israelis on a bus. Robert's answer to my tanka was how someone he refers to as "you" could be so vain as to think he (Robert) had put his daughter on a shelf so that the "you" would not have to dust it. I decided after exchanging twenty-five poems not to continue the project. Now I think that was a mistake because a tanka poet has the right to create his poems in any way he wishes.

What we have now is Robert Wilson's *Jack Fruit Moon* in which he writes his own tanka and follows it with a haiku. The result is the creation of a remarkable world unlike anything seen in tanka and haiku all these centuries. The book is filled with unusual images that make us feel we are experiencing a surrealist world. To cite a few examples: "she sweeps/morning into/piles.../a cockroach fingering/prayer beads"—"in darkness/his limbs grow/flowers" —"starless night.../bulacan scented/armpits/chasing spider/monkeys in drag" A glossary appears at the end of the book in which the many Filipino words the poet uses are defined.

What seems to have happened in this amazing book filled with images never seen on sea or land is that the rationalism of the world is turned upside down or is sent whirling as on an endless merry-go-round. I have Robert's permission to inform readers he has been suffering from postwar-traumatic-stress-syndrome from Vietnam all these years. Fifty-nine now, Robert went to Vietnam at eighteen and saw all the horrors, contradictions, sufferings, cruelties, irrationalities of that horrible unpopular war. He still suffers from nightmares, sleeplessness, and hates crowds and closed-off areas. Several of the poems make references to Vietnam: "the flies/hovering above me/could be the/soldiers I sold/my umbrella to"; "my dreams, in/pieces like shards/of light at/ dawn, inching across/a narrow rope bridge"—

At first we may feel that Robert is playing with us, enjoying all the contradictions and unexpected connections he is making. But as we read on, we can see that he has created a world in which he sympathizes with the working poor (he now lives in the Philippines), the peanut and cigarette and fish and charcoal vendors, sellers of fish paste, rice field workers, a universe of the struggling who go about their tasks in these poems without asking for our sympathy ("on the laborer's/back, a thousand/tiny suns"). We feel the bare qualities of these lives that go on without the usual complaints of American culture even though violence makes its appearance. In addition to a nature of skyscapes, moons, stars, winds, clouds, vegetation, forests, flowers, there are crawling creatures in homes and dreams and sand. There is empathy in these outpourings, awareness of another world beyond our usual experiences.

When I asked Robert why he had used tanka and then haiku juxtaposed against one another, he told me he had been writing "strings" (my invented word) for years, and it seemed right for a tanka to be followed by a haiku. The result is a poetry that expands the freedom of tanka and haiku as open forms.

One final poem: "it's as if/i fell out of my/own dream/sideways into Dali's/surrealistic toreador"—

Sanford Goldstein
Atellib House
Shibata, Japan

Preface

WRITING sometime around 1800, the Japanese scholar-poet Tachibana Nankei offered that *haiku*—which he referred to by the earlier name for the genre, *haikai*—had reached its zenith with Matsuo Bash ō and was doomed to decline. Since then, many other writers, too, have predicted the imminent end of *haiku*—and also of *tanka*, the other prominent form of traditional Japanese poetry. But the nay-sayers have been proved wrong; both forms are still healthy, by any standard—in Japanese, but also in English and other languages. A recent anthology of *haiku* in the Everyman's Library Pocket Poets series even includes poems by a number of poets writing in English. For reasons I will not enumerate here, I cannot wholeheartedly recommend that volume, but its appearance does serve to prove the point that Nankei got it wrong.

There are many explanations for the continued success of *tanka* and *haiku* in English, not least among them the many labors of pioneers too numerous to mention. But also on the list of explanations is a new electronic medium—the world-wide web, which has played and will continue to play a major role in the fate of what used to be called "traditional" Japanese poetry, facilitating kinds of publication and correspondence that were not really possible before. Paper journals still appear of course, as I believe they should. (Those who forecast the end of the book are also mistaken, I hope; there is just something about the look and feel of paper . . .) But the most prominent journals are now mostly available in digital form, which allows for a world-wide circulation for which one can only be grateful.

One of the finest websites in the field is *Simply Haiku: A Quarterly Journal of Japanese Short Form Poetry*, owned and edited by Robert Wilson. Like so many in the past, Wilson deserves applause for hours of labor sustaining an enterprise that probably brings little in the way of financial reward. The poems, translations, essays, reviews, scholarly articles contribute greatly to the health of the discourse.

It goes without saying that Robert is a poet himself, with a number of publications to his credit. In every way, *Simply Haiku* reveals the sensibility of a poet, along with the discipline of an educator. His latest book is a solid contribution to his own body of work and to the field of English-language *haiku* and *tanka*—what he calls, "short form" poetry.

JAPANESE poetry is a poetry of place—of landscape and cityscape; of earth, sea, and sky; and especially of natural spaces that border on human spaces—gardens, parks, and so on. One result of the expansion of the form is that we now see images from Australia, Bulgaria, London, and Paris. Robert Wilson lives in the Philippines, and the poems in this book, which are organized in a sequence of alternating five-line and three-line formats, are rich with the imagery of that place—natural, human, and semi-imaginary, adding up to a curious mix of the real and the surreal, whose forces manage to maintain a proper balance.

There is much apostrophe and even more personification in these poems, which puts the poet into his landscapes and mindscapes in an intimate way. And in other ways too the poems put the poet along borders, sometimes as an observer, sometimes as a participant in what is going on "out there." The world the poems present is a porous one where people and things drift on breezes, pass through each other, dance around each other, or merge into sparkling scenes that often begin in quotidian reality but end up—well, somewhere else.

wide-eyed
watching sequels
under
a blanket
stitched with stars

the neighbor boy's
cry, shepherding
clouds

The book is full of stars, moons, clouds, showers, and their earth-bound counterparts—mangos, jack fruit, fish markets, and all kinds of people, old and young, ceaselessly chattering, juggling, hawking, chopping, sometimes sleeping, gazing, dreaming. Some of the more colorful images of the book—the spider monkeys, carabao, bananas, egrets, herons, jeepneys, coconut palms, snails, flies, snakes, peddlers, fishermen, laborers, shrimp spirits, carp, and hordes of bugs, from mosquitos and ants to cicadas and the ubiquitous cockroach—obviously situate the author in the Philippines, but the world he creates is also a larger place, a place with cosmic borders.

This is not to say, however, that Bashō or later Japanese poets writing in *tanka* or *senryū* or *ky ōka* would not recognize Robert's poems as articulations in some way connected to their poetics. Some of Robert's *haiku*, in particular, are successful at capturing moments in ways familiar to anyone who has read the classics of that genre. But perhaps the word "capture" does not suffice, for what these poems do is to allow us to witness something—something recognizable, but distinctive and unexpected—coming into being in words.

the distance
between trees
summer rain

humid night . . .
her address on a crumpled
piece of paper

are you tongue
tied, cicada?
you repeat yourself!

To experienced readers these poems need no explication. The craft they evince is an old one, which is not to say one that is in any way easy to master.

There are other poems in the book, however, that one is less prepared for. Some I would call ruminative. They ask questions—or rather, present the poet or his speakers as asking questions, often questions with no clear answers.

young leaves . . .
i look for myself
among them

ant, there is
more to me than
a giant foot!

where did you
come from this
time, rain?

where do worms
go at night when the sky
is blanketed
with doubt, and raindrops
take the place of stars?

Finally, some poems present extravagant metaphor that reveals a love
of verbal (and maybe mental?) play:

fleeing
nightfall, the still-borne
voices of
children etched in
stagnant ponds

watching an
ember whisper
like a
boy scout on leave
from his senses

These are poems that choose to *be* rather to *mean*, perhaps. I find them
less impressive than many of the others, but such things are a matter
of taste. And I have to admit that one of my favorite poems is one
that offers a metaphor I can't claim to "interpret" but love anyway.

i settle with
the dust, a pile
of leaves
swept away
into tall whispers

What is a "tall whisper"? I don't know. I'm not sure that I care. I just love the words and don't feel inclined to produce any jargon or psycho-babble to explain myself. My hope is that someday I may hear a tall whisper, and that's enough. And if it only happens in a poem, that will be fine with me.

Steve Carter
Chair and Professor, Department of Asian Languages, Stanford University

What can I say? I think outside of the box. I'm not your average bear and never will be. I was born in downtown Los Angeles. In less than a year I'll be 60. I came into the world on Friday the 13th. I live on french press coffee and have a mind that works a mile a minute. Who am I? I used to think I came from Venus but then again, it's none of your business. Understand my poetry and you'll understand me. Good luck said the thin man with a coat full of watches. I'm a loaner, a koan, a hollow man streaking into your cerebellum NAKED! I'm not captain this or a sought after that, a great pretender without the platters. I live in the Philippines. I don't attend conferences. I fly on the wings of whisper above the Wonderland Amusement Park in search of the great Chalupa, forgetful of time, writing poetry like a mad man when I'm not dashing through books like an even madder mad man, the wind in my pocket, political correctness hanging from the tailpipe of a 57 Chevie lowrider with vibrasonic sound and the requisite dingle balls. La la bamba! Oh, can you tell? I have service related PTSD (post traumatic stress syndrome) contracted in 1968 during the Vietnam War. And after the war, I came home to an even greater war, the one between minds and dictates, a surrealistic journey without the pillow, Jack Kerouac drinking himself to death, Coltrane on his last lap, Ginsberg before he discovered three piece suits, Tim Leary speaking about nothing, his mind on another planet, Elvin Bishop wearing a straw hat and overalls, psychedelic this and marijuana that, the whole country blowing eggs, shedding blood, having babies, carrying signs. I've laid in my own vomit struggling to keep my sanity, and watched the walls before me melt. Oops, I forgot to tell you, I led anti-war demonstrations, discovered church, was a friend of Rick Warren, became a minister, a Fuller Brush man, newspaper man, weight-loss counselor, toy salesman, and a teacher for throw-away kids, the ones others were too lazy to teach and wouldn't, their hearts on leave from their senses, talking smack about students and their parents in the lunchroom over donuts. How did I end up the owner and managing editor of *Simply Haiku*, which in my not so humble opinion is one of the world's premier Japanese short form poetry journals? French Press Coffee? Nada! I believe in what I'm doing, dream the impossible dream, don't like the word, NO, and think tanka, haiku, and senryu are paths to walk down, not a walk through gollywood. I'm starving for the truth whatever that is or isn't, and don't have time to stop on go and collect $200. Japanese short form poetry is the cadillac of poetry and I've written free verse, sonnets, and had a thing for Ogden Nash poems as a pre-pubescent second baseman. There is no end, no beginning, we are and we're not, dashing in and out of the echo of bells and frogs jumping into whatever is the opposite of what ersatz translators say it is . . . got a migraine yet? Read on . . .

JACK FRUIT MOON

return me
dragon to the
elephant
grass field of
too much time

pour me into a
chalice of sun . . .
day moon!

watching
winter slip
past me
into a gaggle
of shadow

late night . . .
bbq-ing clouds
on a spit

Jack FruitM oon

wide-eyed
watching sequels
under
a blanket
stitched with stars

later i'll
pour you into a
teacup moon

that far off
look in your eyes . . .
a thousand
roosters caught
between bouts

dried blood . . .
and the nearness
of dreams

is that you
sitting on the
star above
me crawling out
of a dream?

late morning . . .
that rice field
smile

walking past
videoke bars
and vendors
pretending it's
just another night

Distilling
winter; the echo
between thighs

Jack FruitMoon

how can i
stare at my
reflection
knowing you're on
the other end?

those wings ...
breathing the space
before dawn

warm pancit . . .
she dances with a
dog in her
sleep, sniffing his
reflection

humid day . . .
the wail of a
young girl's brush

those wings ...
breathing the space
before dawn

robert d. wilson

Jack Fruit Moon

the ripples
she nuzzles from
dreams, and a
lizard glued to
the moon's backside

sipping coffee
in the absence
of mirrors

i saw
their maid under
the table,
piecing together
mirrors . . .

morning breeze . . .
she plucked me
from the stars

she sweeps
morning into
piles . . .
a cockroach fingering
prayer beads

musty morning . . .
shadows pretending
to work

what to her
are the peaks of song,
the prayers of
dawn, a woman
bowing to mud gods?

her raspy voice,
a rope bridge
straddling dawn

Jack FruitMoon

upriver
dolphins dance in
a cup
full of stars . . .
singing water

brown water . . .
the stillness of
winter

singing wind . . .
half dressed bargirls
dueling dawn
with nokia
cellphone swords...

lucky rat,
a year is named
for you!

pulling up
stakes, she sang out
of tune with
a shot glass
full of mirrors

chattering teeth . . .
the whistle
of bamboo

she sings to
me in the morning
between stars . . .
an elephant
walking backwards

dragonflies . . .
a field full
of snails!

chanting stones . . .
he'd never
kissed
a woman
like her before

the hemline of
clouds breathing
our dance

dancing lights . . .
she asked me more
than once if
i wanted her drunk,
the shoreline writhing

in darkness
his limbs grow
flowers

i skirt
around a puddle,
carried by
dragons into
morning

reaching into
the dragon's mouth . . .
muttered words

running lights . . .
in the front seat of
a jeepney
staring at the
shape of her legs

midnight . . .
that light in the charcoal
seller's house

Jack Fruit Moon

he sleeps through
noon on a cement
slab scented
with peanuts and
stale memories

tilling clouds . . .
the peanut vendor's
noon

in the wild
west of the night,
the cry
of a cockroach
clothed in ants

late night . . .
a lizard
clutching shadows

sundown . . .
an old woman
scooping
fish paste into
recycled bottles

dripping water . . .
the hoarse cry of
a motorbike

another
jeepney ride into
the carabao's
belly . . . a
bevy of toes

mirrors
severed by an
egret's wing . . .

Jack Fruit Moon

dancing with
lights; your nipples
lead me to
the bed we broke last
night in a haiku

humid night . . .
the tricycle
driver's pocket . . .

ebb tide . . .
half a world
away my
reflection sings
to you in mirrors

speak to me,
mountain, of mornings
draped in pearls

Jack FruitMoon

i follow
you into dark
crevices
dampened with a
young man's smile

new moon . . .
the spent shell of
a cockroach

she is
hocking fast food
on the curb,
spewing dreams
into a cellphone

your fingers,
a trellis
courting spring

she bartered
with me for the
dreams her
smile couldn't buy . . .
jeepney horns!

look,
a day moon
juggling trees!

on his back
the peanut seller
categorizes
yesterday with
a toothless grin

listen,
whispers surfing
waves

Jack FruitM oon

if it weren't
for you, i would
be sorting
papers inside of
a dry grass spring yawn

late afternoon . . .
the stench of empty
stalls

nara wood
embers writhe in
smoke
leavened with her
mother's last breath

ripe mangos. ..
she walks past me
in a hurry!

you told me
you didn't have
long to live,
the dacshund on your
lap, chasing clouds

nightfall . . .
plucking lights in a
windowless room

the first wind
of autumn and
still no moon
to carry me
into winter

dried shrimp . . .
the rustle of a
vendor sleeping

Jack FruitMoon

what will you
do at night when
the wind sings
to you in circles
and clouds chase dogs?

sunrise . . .
watching the fish
seller's hands

the dried fish
vendor before
dawn, slaying
wind mills with a
make-shift swatter . . .

late morning . . .
the little girl's salted
egg smile

Jack FruitMoon

fishermen
sewing twilight
into the
bowels of an
overcast night

humid morning . . .
the egg seller
and her mirror

autumn mist . . .
a fish farmer
staring at
the tail end of
a paper moon

mid-morning . . .
a wet market vendor
sweeping fish scales

rain saunters
on our roof muffling
half-formed words
played later in
a second wind

a full moon . . .
she steadies
her gait

she talks to
him as if I
don't exist . . .
a cacophony
of bird song

good friday . . .
nothing to do
but sleep

Jack FruitM oon

drinking
brandy chased with
grape juice . . .
the movie we
forgot to watch

holy week . . .
a long line
of shadows

advent . . .
she walked past me
with a limp
into the
jeepney's belly

bulacan . . .
the moon sitting
in its own waste

the stench of
water staggering
through an
old man's legs . . .
ebony moon

blinking lights
stare at me with
a mango smile

she plucked
every star; brown
fingers
gessoed with a
carabao's contrail

of course he
lays there . . .
jack fruit moon!

Jack FruitMoon

summer moon . . .
he asks me to
drink with him
beneath a string
of colored lights

that look, last
night . . . a dark sky
bearing gifts

late night . . .
watching the girl
she wouldn't
be, fold stars into
paper-strip me's

tonight i'll
dream of you . . .
smelling blossoms

that river . . .
everytime i
pass it, i
cover my nose
and think of her

nursing a headache . . .
the peanut vendor
and dawn

our son gets
circumcised next
week, his
teddy bear at home
fawning yesterday

late morning
the moon upstairs
in our bedroom

Jack FruitMoon

more than an
old woman's hand
steeping tea,
the song of tricycles
searching dawn

barking dogs . . .
the neighbors
singing karaoke

where do you
go, cockroach, when
night has
nowhere to hide
and dust is dust?

watching the
sweat on your brow
write haiku

like cockroaches
venders slip out of
their shadows
into a night
breathing jeepneys

sunday morning . . .
lolos eating lugaw
from plastic bags

she said all
she has to do
is eat, and
looks the part, her
fanny towing shadows

summer's breath . . .
a child begging
for pesos

Jack FruitMoon

will she still
smell like fish when
night swallows
her, the rice in her
veins reaching skyward?

stifling heat . . .
sinking into a bed
moist with morning

there you are
midway through a
dream, telling
me the moon is
made of paper

humid night . . .
fanning herself in front
of tatay's casket

heavy rain . . .
the television
in our
living room
mouthing godzilla

sundown . . .
the chit-chat
of chopsticks

i hear your
cry half a world
away and
think of dolphins
caught in a trawler's net

starless night . . .
the chatter of
prostitutes

Jack FruitM oon

a cooler
night than last; the
low drone of
motorbikes and
pubescent girls

sudden showers . . .
a rat scurries under
the pool table

dancing in
each other's eyes . . .
a stand of
naga trees garlanded
with heavy mist

the clarity
of a smile dipped
in pollen

your silence
speaks to me in
tongues . . .
the jungle a
cathedral singing light

twilight dusk . . .
carp jump out of
the lazy man's belly

they play cards
on the floor of the
wet market,
sandwiched between
the cries of fish

slicing fish on
a cement slab . . .
chatting knives

Jack FruitM oon

next to me
in the jeepney,
a woman
clutches her cellphone
like a stray lover

the balut vendor . . .
an echo
splicing darkness

in twos
young girls ply their
bodies like
relay racers
jumping the gun

a deep growl . . .
the tricycle driver
threading dawn

what keeps them
here, this graveyard
of dust and
strewn paper, a
sister to the ox

swatting flies,
the fish seller
at dawn

a tricycle
driver wearing
a white mask
passes me on
his way to hell

coughing into
her apron, the
meycauayan river

Jack FruitMoon

he pees on
the cemetery wall,
his bulbous
stub jiggling
with every shake

passing over the
meycauayan river . . .
summer moon

what will they
do when the wind
replaces
their breath, and leaves
flail like dying soldiers?

a parade of
stone pillars . . .
the flower seller

where is the
song, the chatter,
the wisps of
children holding
court in cement stalls?

swept by the
jeepney's tail . . .
dancing rice

overcast night . . .
she eats dinner
at the
table without me,
fencing leftovers

boredom . . .
a vendor stirring
himself

Jack FruitM oon

twilight. . .
passersby paint
the walls of
the cemetery
with shadows

wet market . . .
slicing a
mackerel's cry

noon stillness . . .
waiting for the
sun to
slither across
the stagnant lake

the heat!
a small chested girl
squeezing mangos

sipping
buko in the shade,
an old man
nursing the boy
he used to be

clapping fish . . .
knowing they'll be
in today's newspaper

summer heat . . .
an empty-eyed
woman plods
past me into the
gecko's mouth

high noon . . .
a shirtless man
plowing the sun

we finished
lunch feeling the
air for words
to bind loose clouds
into clumps of now

a steady gait . . .
with blossoms
taped to her jacket

a young girl
juggles silence
like a toy
in a water-
filled bauble

night poured
stars into a cup
and stuttered

Jack FruitMoon

her breath
treads the depths of
dawn like
a plastic duck
without bath water

selling cigarettes,
a vendor caught
between clouds

dicing shallots . . .
our son in the
next room
showing off the toys
he'll leave behind

potted plants . . .
all that's left of
yesterday

cutting an
onion against
the grain . . .
her sandals one
size too small

christmas lights . . .
a line in front
of the inn

they talk
behind my back
like flies
who think they are
a carabao

cicadas
emptying themselves
of words

Jack FruitMoon

starless night . . .
bulacan scented
armpits
chasing spider
monkeys in drag

she acts
as if darkness
was more than
a lover walking
on telephone lines

squeeze me
into a plastic bag
and sip

will the sun
continue to
greet me like
the resident of
a nursing home?

60

join me in a
sinigang night of
straggling whispers

i long for
water to return
me to the
quiet mother gave
me in darkness

late afternoon . . .
waiting for the
sun's demise

the dust from
my sandals came
from america
in installments . . .
your tipsy breath

Jack FruitMoon

bulacan . . .
the stacatto of
stench and bone

i don't need
a photo of you
to call night
a lover, to harvest
stars with a plastic scythe

the sweetness
of small mangoes
. . . and time!

a jack fruit
moon! i can watch
her all night
stuffing coconuts
into empty pockets

a light sleeper,
the moon, polishing
rice paddies

water
clinging to lines
without
plastic bubbles
and condoms

paper fish . . .
massaging the rich
man's trousers

where's the fish,
the shrimp, words playing
hopscotch in
bubbles and clear
water thoughts?

Jack FruitMoon

in a thousand
years, crab, your . . .
krinkled smile

this mud-caked
carabao, her
grunts on an
altar God has
no patience for

squinting sun . . .
a pregnant girl squats
on the newspaper

i'm bored,
shotetsu...let's
break mirrors
and drink from
plastic teacups

lola cross-stitches
sundown in an
oversized dress

she waddles
past me like a
duck courting
ripples . . . her
porcelain beak

early evening . . .
a bamboo fawning
clouds

bamboo . . .
her shoots glean
droplets
from fields too drunk
to remember

Jack Fruit Moon

late night . . .
a shortage
of leaves

and sunlight,
your serpentine
smile
fools no one during
a shortage of rice

watching
the sun wring
itself out

beneath your
bra, a storybook
princess
staring shyly at
her reflection

humid night . . .
a minnow polishing
stones

a faint light . . .
the murmur of
men chalking
pool cues into
butterfly wings

crablets for sale
in small crypts
. . . summer wind

chatter
sashays down-river
like a
fat women
feigning youth

a mother to
flies, this mango
turned inward

this rain . . .
longing to be a
street corner
washed of grease
and still chatter

"opo" . . .
as if it'll make
a tree grow!

                    *** "yes sir" in tagalog

she listens
on the other side
of the fence
to a cold moon
coughing up phlegm

her bouquet
dressing a new
soldier's grave

the look she
gave me when i
handed her
a bag of peanuts
nailed to the sky

fresh leaves . . .
a mango measuring
time

twilight dawn . . .
she saw me on
a postage
stamp slapping
the moon's backside

Jack Fruit Moon

young leaves . . .
watching a
mango grow

muffled cries
tear dawn from
my fingers . . .
and i think of you,
wrestling cloud dragons

sundown . . .
listening to a
dull horizon

i wake up
to the early morning
stench of
waste water, your
bra unbuttoned

mid-autumn . . .
squash prepare
to die

almost 60,
this gnarled tree reminds
me of an old
man riding a bicycle
in his underwear

moon-bound . . .
words flutter on
a moth's wings

i sip your words
when i'm troubled,
like a
baby suckling
mother's breasts

Jack FruitMoon

fainting lights . . .
the yawn of a
distant highway

she came back
in a few minutes
talking about
a man with poop
on his shorts

young leaves
painting an old
man's shadow

she stood on
the moon and stretched
her arms,
a top heavy egret
bending backwards

Jack FruitM oon

a man child
skipping stones across
the forest

gone are the
trees, their laughter
in the
morning sifting
roadside rice

look, heron's
vending dawn in
a white apron!

the night sky
reminds ant of a
hungry queen;
the patter of feet,
a locust's cry!

the day moon
dulled by a
woman's tears

in my
pocket, the granite
smile of
a windblown night
pawing autumn

humid night . . .
listening to
stars giggle

that yawn . . .
the cha cha of
moths
bouncing off
christmas lights

Jack FruitMoon

a fawn leaving
night with stars
on her tail

twin moons . . .
her eyes follow
me home
in the caption
above my head

moon-bound . . .
this dusting of
pollen

he fishes
inside of a
still born moon
mumbling words he
can't remember

still water . . .
the stench of a
newborn moon

the wind this
morning hastened
my dream,
towing me in
circles around the moon

turning myself
inside out . . .
humid night

no longer
can i suckle
darkness,
the moon turning
tricks with a passerby

Jack FruitMoon

hyacinth . . .
wading through other
men's dreams

chasten me
with stars, our backs turned
inside out
like paper dragons on
leave from their senses

without bamboo
there are no birds
to sweep the wind

this breeze
and the song sung
on limbs
by small leaves
pretending to be birds

this water
and the jeepney
i've become

gliding
between jeepneys
through strips
of cloud and
mail order brides

in the water
a young woman
rinsing dreams

whatever
usual is, the
clink clink clink
of crystal they
cannot afford

Jack FruitMoon

a pond sobbing
on the other side
of the grass

what are
clouds and long walks
to the
vendor nursing
stone children?

after the rain,
the onset of slugs . . .
and whistles

ants carry
pieces of me
into a
story i'll write
later between moons

calling the
wind autumn
and coughing

lantern-less night . . .
sounds waiting
for a line to
draw them out
of black pools

just a few
stars and a boy
talking to flames

moon viewing . . .
time speeds past me
mumbling
something about
a tea party

mosquito.
your wings, too,
speak godliness

water sings
to me in the
quiet
between echoes . . .
dancing lights

rambutan . . .
a deformed man
inside the temple

as if i
had anything to
do with this
turn, a gray wind
carving totems

cockroach . . .
the bleating of a
gray sky

i pull you
into morning
skipping
moons across
stagnant ponds

young leaves . . .
i look for myself
among them

i settle with
the dust, a pile
of leaves
swept away
into tall whispers

Jack FruitM oon

trees . . .
i reach past them
into heaven

speak to me
wind, when night
has no more
stars, and the moon
looks at me cross-eyed

bananas . . .
as if unveiling them
will change me!

follow me,
tree, into the book
i'm writing,
your gnarled trunk
thick with seed

at night
she bathes me . . .
apricot moon

her talons
carry my heart
into clouds
thickened with an
old man's dreams

a poof of wind . . .
the questions it
poses to a soldier

no one told
me the enemy
was a mirror
floating beneath
rice paddies

Jack FruitMoon

into the rain
the sadness of
worms thirsting

all that's left
of blossoms clothing
dung . . .
the swirl of wind
wooing autumn

now carried in
the pinchers of
a cockroach

vietnam . . .
the footsteps of
godzilla
and
carousel horses

summer evening . . .
the chatter of
spider webs

i step
into this tree
sprouting leaves,
knowing they will
fall and wither

brown water . . .
watching death float
between my legs

i join you
monkey, in the
mountains,
thinking the world
away . . . and quiet

Jack FruitMoon

thrice divorced . . .
can i join
you buddha?

tasting
chocolate . . . the
stretch between
trees, a rope bridge
made of petals

the lullaby
of waves, and no
walls

wishing my
knee would heel, the
summer sky
steeping in a
cold gray broth

high noon . . .
listening to shadows
lap water

summer skies
girdled with coco-
nut leaves
and a patch
of gray hair

speak louder,
mirror, the water
beneath you

in bed
listening to rats scurry
across the
tin roof of an
old war movie

Jack FruitMoon

summer rain . . .
the coconut leaf
girdled sky

colored lights
plunge me into
a darkness
hollow with
never enough

harvest moon . . .
spilling seed in the
jack fruit patch

the blush of
mangos waiting
to be picked
in stalls scented
with fish paste

another
humid night watching
mangos blush

your fingers
speak of long days
and short nights
planting moons in
a snail's lair

at midnight,
a dead mouse lighting
lanterns

acquiescing
to sanguine moons,
the beetle
on my son's chest
chewing stillness

Jack FruitMoon

sharing heat
with a handful
of water

the still-life
standing in a
pool of stars
listening to
an egret's breath . . .

leaving summer . . .
a coconut palm
dripping clouds

where did the
frog jump when the
sun rose and
the old pond sailed
into thought?

the distance
between trees . . .
summer rain

is this how
the worm feels
drowning in
his own bed
between storms?

another lizard
dressed as a dragon . . .
warm winds

voices in
my head scamper
like small
children in a trailer
park stealing stars

Jack FruitMoon

steeped in
clouds, the stone
faced vendor

and for no
reason i gaze
upon the
absence of words
vending blossoms

between seasons,
the sky
shouting wolf

for no reason
i sit on the
curb watching
silence jump in
to old ponds

with dengue,
a woman waking
darkness

every day
she fans the dried
fish she sells
to neighbors
in newsprint jackets

breathing clouds
into flat seas . . .
night sickness

halo
halo women
walk through me
clutching plastic
bags of vinegar

Jack FruitMoon

long day . . .
crouching woman
talking snails

back turned,
he pees on the
cemetery
wall, a mime
draped in summer

the water running
through my house . . .
coughing blood

the song-less
wail of swollen
bellies
parading down
c. molina street

climbing out of
winter, tree limbs
calling favors

a wisp of
wind? my mother's
chanel
clinging to coffee
cups is every room

the water
in my ear stutters . . .
nightmare!

chicken wings
cooked in black bean
sauce
hobble downwind
on crutches

Jack FruitMoon

cooling me,
the sky breathing
threats

the child
inside of me
nurses a
plastic bag
filled with soda

another warm
night listening to
old dogs die

nursing a
an injured knee . . .
in the
corner of my eye,
a dog lapping flies

father waits
for me in a field
bleeding words

the flies
hovering above me
could be the
soldiers i sold
my umbrella to

the rice field
inside of me
chastening soldiers

eggless
her reflection
swims away
from me into
handfuls of thought

Jack FruitMoon

twilight dawn . . .
arm-wrestling an
absentee moon

the spoiled
milk in this carton
has no
regard for the
contents of my soul

sunrise;
the brush of
a sunflower

the rat on
our roof last night
doesn't know
i'm naked in
bed writing poetry

late night . . .
the moon swinging
from a tree limb

night sweats . . .
our neighbor yells
at his
wife between
mosquito bites

dengue fever . . .
a runner
passing shadows

your memory
grabbed me from
behind
clasping a paper
clip bracelet

Jack FruitM oon

peeing on
mosquito eggs . . .
autumn memory

bowing to
cockroaches, the
sticky back
of a carabao
blackened with words

friday evening . . .
a monitor lizard
pushing lights

as if autumn
can remember
the sun, and
leaves ladle clouds
into bowls of light

Jack FruitMoon

what is it, this
night between lines,
speaking cricket?

watching
darkness wet your
lips, clasping
clumps of cloud
clumps of cloud

late summer
and still a fever
to haunt you

your blood
refuses to
be categorized
pulsing fears into
tightly wrapped words

your bite
waits for me in
a stagnant pond

infinite stars,
and like the words
i pluck from
darkness, waiting
to be breathed

the snake
writhing in tall grass,
has no father

tossing pebbles
into the clearness
you offered
me when hydrangea
wore raincoats

foamfish . . .
their still-water
contrails

fleeing
nightfall, the still-borne
voices of
children etched in
stagnant ponds

like rain, a
parade of candles
skirting summer

the trail
of wind trailing
wind,
trailing wind . . .
summer rain

late in life,
a woman chewing
leaves

the rain
inside your heart
has nowhere
to settle when
petals court darkness

the lugaw cook
reads her fortune on
clumps of morning

why do you
insist on forging
petals
into swords no
one can wield?

Jack FruitMoon

in the caption
above me, a sky rocket
lipsincing flies

bugs from
the rain-soaked sky,
lodge in my brain
like soldiers ducking
mortar shells

laundry soap
and a young mother's
dreams

a halo
halo woman leans
into the
clothing she swore
she'd never wash

Jack FruitM oon

lingering,
a day moon
spewing moths

the bugs in
my bed think i'm
their lover
pushing darkness
through wet windows

high noon . . .
eating halo halo on
the carabao's back

somewhere in
your coffee cup
a giant
wave drags me
out of complacence

the vendor cutting
chicken with words . . .
starless night

held up by
crutches, this old trunk
contemplates
the leaves of
a thousand autumns

smooth stones . . .
the coolness of
their stare

a dream?
the neighbor's
baby
tossing peacocks
into metal maws

Jack FruitMoon

rain's yawn
stretched morning
across mountains

trees
fiord what used to
be grass
under a rope bridge
frayed with silence

the clink clink
of dinnerware in the
fish farmer's wake

i sat with
you during your
pregnancy
waiting my
turn to die

milking noon
for a thousand words . . .
sanctuary!

the jungle
i long for
tattooed
on my mother's
belly with milk

flowers
waiting for a
flower's stillness

how long will
these walls stare
through me
into the neighbor's
glass eye?

Jack FruitMoon

steeping the
sameness of autumn . . .
traffic cop!

morning stillness
an egret chasing
clouds
in a field
of mirrors

the emptiness
of leaves
flailing autumn

for me, the
scars of words tacked
to my brain
like petals pressed
between pages

my injured
leg, your wings . . .
taunting icarus!

my dreams, in
pieces like shards
of light at
dawn, inching across
a narrow rope bridge

at dusk, the
hiccup of a
lost whale

you gave
birth to me in
the latter
half of dawn, a
seagull chiding stars

shortened day . . .
the water asks for
no answers

free-falling
into an ulam pot
with small flies . . .
have you heard
of condoms?

the night moon . . .
sampaguita
ilang ilang

she made
sandwiches with
a maid's smile . . .
a straw broom,
stretching canyons

cockroaches
are early risers . . .
jack fruit moon!

i follow a
bayawak into
the forest
of a jack fruit moon,
bending words

late night . . .
the pungent odor
of patis

to become
a poet, i walk
across
McArthur highway
pocketing lights

august rains
pass me on their
way to hell

beneath the
bridge, a hundred
lost words
blackened with algae
. . . autumn wind

under the bridge . . .
black-faced words
scribbling summer

i hear you
river, breathing
water . . .
the prayers of soldiers
the prayers of fish

mango moon
the day before my wife's
masectomy

a smart
worker, the cockroach,
staring
at me through the
cracks of dawn

late night . . .
the neighbor girl
breast-feeding dolls

sitting on
the toilet without
a seat,
soldering what's
left of summer

Jack Fruit Moon

rotting fruit . . .
and still the long
line of ants

what is night
in a city
without lights,
without birds, a
clown to step into?

autumn mist . . .
a tricycle in the
tree above me

where will you
be the latter part
of tonight when
cockroaches peer up
at you from their meals?

a minah bird
on my dresser
. . . autumn mist

longing for
morning, a thick
white fog
dances in circles
around my ankles

endless summer . . .
a cockroach
melding silence

wary, the
feral cat staring
out of the
broken window in
the hospital ward

Jack FruitMoon

tonight,
a shooting star
stretching dreams

a shooting
star races past
me on its
way to another
man's pocket

always summer . . .
drinking from a
stagnant pond

what is winter
to patients waiting
in line to
use the hospital
ward's one toilet?

this heat . . .
and everything i
take for granted

drink with me
from petals filled with
dreams; the clang
of metal; the stench of
a dying man's urine

no birds
beneath the taho
vendor's cry

somewhere the
'use to' of birds
and lizards
rising from
magazine covers

Jack FruitM oon

fencing summer
with a can of
insect spray

in hiding,
blackbirds swooping
words
into small lumps
of gaseous clouds

at dusk,
the heat splaying
men's souls

i wait for
my operation
in the
company of cockroaches,
listening to cats yeow

jack fruit moon . . .
the dance of moths in
a kitten's paw

dogs barking
from their cages
at rats . . .
scampering
to distant moons

the neighbor boy's
cry, shepherding
clouds

if only i
could grab their wombs
and show them
a place by the
stream, chanting dawn

Jack FruitMoon

like summer,
morning sang to
her and shriveled

your sandals
follow me home
from the
hospital with a
cheshire cat smile

the brown
water smiles of children
splashing dusk

out of the
quiet, a moon too
drunk to peel
back the night . . .
pees through clouds

Jack FruitM oon

summer hands
pick lice from a
little girl's head

at midnight,
a gentle wind
raking rows
in the bargirl's
black tresses

brown water
children splashing
carabao

you apologized
for having small breasts,
offered me
a can of
over-priced fruit juice

the flies in
the palengke
eye me greedily

once
upon a dream,
my daughter
stared at an
egret and quacked

a blue sky . . .
and no gulls
seeding clouds

i ride through
the bowels of the
beast today
on a tricycle
juggling coconuts

Jack FruitMoon

stay the night
with me on strips
of moon . . .

i heard the
voices of vendors
swatting flies . . .
the echo of wings
the cadence of legs

nirvana . . .
a stream of
nervous bubbles

a nervous
man speeds through my
brain in a
wheelchair to keep
from going crazy

mid-summer . . .
the same man
pees on the same wall

the young maid
washing laundry
in my
heart, pauses to
. . . snatch a dream

sunrise . . .
the flowerless women
of C. Molina Street

in the middle
of the highway
in bataan, a
WILD man walks nude
through pirated movies

Jack FruitMoon

she melts like
a candle into my
collage of words

the morning
sky hovers over
me, weighted
down with the gray
eyes of vendors

late night. . .
the world turned
inside out

in a borrowed
still-life, dried fish
lay still
on the vendor's slab,
gulping blanks

a milkfish
swallowing
nightfall

like a durian's
rind, your words speak
sharply, hiding
the foul scent
of envy

in a gray mood,
clouds swatting the
moon's backside . . .

sallow spirits
paint me into
corners they
forgot to fence . . .
hunter's moon

summer morning . . .
stopping to take the
ocean's pulse

in your eyes,
egret, a thousand
more . . .
bowing like straw
dolls to a mirror

late noon . . .
an egret staring
nowhere

summer night . . .
leathery women
walking in
and out of other's
people's dreams

in the field,
dear drinking from
a bowl of moon

if they were
stars, would they see
themselves
as grains of sand,
shifting with the wind?

mirrors plucking
words from brown
water paddies

at dusk,
the child inside
of me stands
beside herons,
gazing at the moon

Jack FruitMoon

on the laborer's
back, a thousand
tiny suns

going into
morning, the brown
water smile
of a planter
seeding clouds

poets looking
for the silence of
leaves not falling

i followed
her into the
quiet, whispering
leaves, trees, and the
birds that never came

the trees too,
speak in tongues . . .
autumn dusk

again and
again the roosters
plead with God
to save them from
armageddon

the emptiness
of words, the echo
of silence . . .

they bite me
and run, the bugs
hiding
beneath my bed
in a child's dream

Jack Fruit Moon

summer's end . . .
an old man picks
his nose

there's so much
i want to learn
before i
pass with the moon
into the milk-fish's mouth

a cold faced
moon selling
dry goods

the house
lizard at dawn
listening to
the nearby flutter
of mosquito wings

your spirit, dog,
has no tail . . .
morning mist

a long day . . .
spirits of dried
shrimp swim
through the vendor's
mind, juggling echos

sunday morning . . .
roosters jousting
tethers

my friends,
towering palm trees,
speak to me
at night in a
raspy whisper

Jack FruitMoon

ant, there is
more to me than
a giant foot!

it comes
and goes, this rain,
like a fair
weather friend on
a drinking binge

late summer . . .
an elderly man
sipping days

exhausted . . .
emptiness caresses
huge rocks
in streams waltzing
through my mind

with closed
eyes, rock, i see a
different you

the water
beneath this ship
. . . and the
emptiness of those
who say they are

autumn . . .
watching a filipina
stuff tacos

fish swim through
me in a hurry
to be dried
and sold to people
clutching plastic bags

Jack FruitMoon

late winter . . .
watching the moon
cross my path

she walked
knee deep in water
to visit
our house above
the floating world

i toss stars
into the bay calling
it nightfall

he gives his
daughter a piggy
back ride
through the dreams
he never had

laguna de bay . . .
tilapia jumping
through dreams

the stillness
of stars
      the bliss
of a
    moon-swept word
falling as
     a blossom
between
    plantings

the charcoal
seller on a night
full of fireflies

Jack FruitMoon

what will you
do when the voices are
no more and
the wind lays silence
at your feet, miming stars?

the t-shirt
above his belly
tilling clouds

i woke up
to the rustle of birds,
of ghosts,
voices that borrow clouds
for bodies, clutching dreams

parting grass
with a snail's
whisper

in my stomach
a bowl of rice . . .
woman bowing
to themselves in
brown water mirrors

cats,
and the winter
they missed

it stopped
raining . . . the frog
in the
hospital ward singing
where he left off

carp in the
restaurant swimming
through echoes

a brother
to the cockroach?
i lay in
my bed at the charity
ward counting cats

eating lugaw
inside a tricycle
driver's belch

moonless night . . .
i carefully wade
through the
water in the charity
ward's one restroom

high noon . . .
longing for the carabao
of their youth

even in
my dreams, the monitor
lizard avoids
me, hiding behind
a fish's shadow

a typhoon!
leaving me breathless
. . . as usual!

my brother
in-law brought a
monitor
lizard into our
home, stacking words

a strong rain . . .
the sadness
of worms

Jack FruitMoon

how sad
the man asking
the beetle
on his bed to
keep him company

monsoon rain . . .
the dance of a
thousand feet

not a hare
but a broken tree
trunk weaving
dreams into
a patchwork quilt

where do
you go, lizard?
the monsoons!

a typhoon
bullies his way across
town, unaware
of the man under the
eaves talking to himself

heavy rain . . .
the pungent scent
of dried fish

where do worms
go at night when the sky
is blanketed
with doubt, and raindrops
take the place of stars?

think about
it moth, dusting
dry moons!

Jack FruitMoon

is this
the sea that holds my
parents ashes;
a cousin to the stars
swimming through moons?

wading through
rain water, a vendor
hawking dry goods

 in my
pocket, a thousand
tiny stars
waiting to be tacked
up on the ceiling

late night . . .
the stillness
settling in

the bamboo's soul . . .
that old man selling
ginger root
on the sidewalk,
siphoning dreams

lites off . . .
a field sprouting
egrets

an umbrella
falls out of the sky
into an
old man's mouth and the
dreams he spat out

morning mist . . .
a vendor salting
his shadow

Jack FruitMoon

it's as if
i fell out of my
own dream
sideways into Dali's
surrealistic toreador

thunder!
same sound,
different father

a leather doll,
she hobbles up and
down the street,
waiting for the key
in her back to break

where did you
come from this
time, rain?

in a dream,
gnus fall off cliffs
onto the
backs of io moths,
straddling icarus

at noon, he
forgets to eat . . .
the peanut vendor

in the
silence between
lines, a
crazy woman
muttering words

end of june . . .
speaking into a
soldier's bones

Jack FruitMoon

the whispers
of bones, the breathing
of angels
transcribing themselves
out of glass windows

the moon,
tonight, a grassy
whisper

i can sleep
now that you have
whispered me
into being . . .
without the stars

at dusk, i watch
the sun wade through
an egret's breath

clouds speed
through me, unmindful
of the moon;
the coolness of breath
the murkiness of dreams

gone are the birds
bamboo spouted . . .
blood soaked moon

and there,
in darkness, shunning
the waking world,
an egret painting words
with his beak

autumn . . .
the uneven song
of a cricket

Jack FruitMoon

you are not
the god you think
you are, a
plastic buddha
turned inside out

as if silence
were enough . . .
the monsoon!

flickering lights . . .
a million stars for
company,
owning darkness
gulping silence

a groaning in the
jungle, that dragon
made of water

juggling words
the circus man
scans the room
looking for shadows
he can swallow

oh, to
categorize a ghost
without wind

water's edge . . .
a thousand thoughts
swirl between
your legs into
darkened crannies

stars, only stars . . .
dusting night
with pollen

Jack FruitMoon

high noon . . .
planters sink into
mirrors
holding copies
of das kapital

june at dusk;
a creek gasping
for water

the sun
walks in circles
tossing
shadows onto
laborer's backs

the first of
july; the same
old sun!

robbers!
they take the sun
away from
me and call it
a waning moon

her shadow
at night, swallowing
moons

as if you
can stop me from
skipping like
a stone across
words, across words

laying down food
you'll never eat . . .
autumn leaves

Jack FruitMoon

he left,
towing shadows
in his wake;
a cousin to
the jigsaw puzzle

summer rain . . .
wading from room
to room

his voice
dances between
canyon walls . . .
a hollow man
a hollow man

summer rain . . .
the echos of
children crying

holding her
baby, she waded
knee deep in
water; sounding what
she thought were dreams

a monitor
lizard squeezing
darkness . . .

you saw through
the looking glass
that wasn't
there into alice's
tea cup, coughing

parting clouds . . .
she waited until
evening

Jack FruitMoon

beneath
my reflection
the same you,
your calloused hands
covered with mud

i eat breakfast
wondering if the
rain has ears

i breathe
the sound of rain
falling, your
footsteps, words
to sip at night

summer rain . . .
words i'm
toying with

look at me
in clumps of cloud
eating dawn
sipping silence
into being

late night . . .
a rat tapping on
the roof

with no one
to talk to at noon
i trace your
breath stretched tautly
across canyon walls

sunday morning . . .
wearing a stained
glass smile

Jack FruitMoon

will you
visit me, a
gust of wind
screeching between
canyon cliffs?

a vendor selling
summer on a stick . . .
humid night

not a
single bird, their
songs nesting
on branches in a
children's lullaby

a poet sweeping
leaves into words ...
morning mist

it's what she
doesn't say that
intrigues me . . .
walking through clouds
with a purse full of stars

a boy fills
his lantern with dreams
. . . chasing fog

between
night and morning
the song
of snails on
their way to work

telling me
to slow down...
cicada song

Jack Fruit Moon

speak to me,
tree, in the still
of morning
when blossoms are
still getting dressed

one day, son,
the sky'll clear . . .
cherry blossoms

what is dirt
when you're a child
straddling
dragons, the sky
raining shrapnel?

short night . . .
filling the space
between blossoms

write with me
a tanka we can
visit later
over hot coffee
and warm semen

casting my line
into a tired look . . .
late summer

past the moon,
clouds speak of you
with a
clothesline smile . . .
clacking bamboo

frolicking stream . . .
a cicada's
sad song

Jack FruitM oon

she looks at
me through a veil
of fruit . . .
i could never be
the buddha sweating

a long day . . .
and a shorter path
to the moon

swimming through
the dragon's bladder
into hell . . .
a pathway lit
with human torches

summer rain . . .
mud dancing through
my toes

a kindred
spirit, the rat ...
on our roof top,
his thin coat lined
with cheap watches

trees bow in
darkness to the
prince of tides

you were there
for me in the
hospital . . .
a butterfly
circling shadows

are you tongue
tied, cicada?
you repeat yourself!

Jack FruitMoon

i woke up
this morning to
a typhoon . . .
a soldier's head
pointing me upriver

birds return me
to the painting they left . . .
summer rain

rising from
a nightmare, i
saw myself
running to the river
dodging bullets

having nowhere
to nest, a bird
treading water

the books in
the crate outside my
home, do they
read me at night
when i'm sleeping?

half the girls
on my street are pregnant,
carrying
boredom to the brim . . .
peanuts: 5 pesos a bag

visit me
tomorrow in my
latest dream;
a young boy tossing stars
into his mother's basket

Jack FruitMoon

summer storm . . .
looking for the
white space

trash piled
up on the side
of the road
like prayers no one
has a need for

autumn mist .. .
birds wait for darkness
to swallow me

stare into
my eyes, lizard,
you'll see
an old man putting
his pants on backward

the palengke . . .
your breath follows
me into autumn

like you,
lizard, i'm bound to
the cage i
was placed in at
birth, feeding dreams

she sees me as
a piece of fruit . . .
autumn wind

orion
looks up at me
from the
tea cup he sleeps
in, wondering

Jack FruitMoon

you sit
alone in america
wandering where
you'll get the money
to purchase eggs

at night
she bathes me like
a baby . . .
sending ripples
down heaven's river

I watch
people from the
sidewalk like
someone in a
Norman Rockwell painting

a young boy
fishes for stars in
heaven's river

Jack FruitMoon

ampalaya . . .
the sincerity
of your words
convincing me
to look deeper

with you, ant,
i stare up at
the stars

I'm getting
older, feeling what
my father
felt when he wore
pointed cowboy boots

a small bird . . .
missing the song I
never heard

that i may
not see you again
is too much
for me to handle . . .
scattered showers

leaves of grass . . .
the faintness of
an egret's breath

i stand with
egrets in a cool
water pool . . .
painting summer
with a cat tail

a dried fish
swimming through
clumps of cloud

Jack FruitMoon

without you
i'd be under
an eave
staring at a
brown paper bag

the gray slumber
of clouds beneath a
summer moon

watching an
ember whisper
like a
boy scout on leave
from his senses

watching
an
ember
whisper
like a
boy scout
on leave
from
his senses

watching an / ember whisper / like a / boy scout on leave / from his senses

autumn . . .
the brown water
smile that isn't

Jack FruitM oon

your song, dog,
lingers like a blues rift
played at dawn
with roosters, toads
and long lost loves

like the moon,
you come and go,
come and go

i woke up
in a cold sweat
from a dream
made in china . . .
dancing with roosters

lanternless night . . .
a woman too old
to dream

the mountain
that isn't there,
crochets
herself at night
into could-have-beens

riding home on
a jeepney . . .
the lullaby of dawn

where can we
go when the monsoon
draws us in,
unwilling to give
up her echo?

like children, the
clouds, racing over
arched backs

Jack FruitMoon

struggling to
find God's face in
humankind,
brother cockroach
lights a joss stick

in the company
of egrets, a calf
lifting its tail

come dawn, in
a pool of vomit . . .
wondering
if i can make it
through the labyrinth

crescent moon . . .
a bar girl stares at
her daughter's photo

tepid air . . .
what good is a
night full of
stars when you are
not one of them

a cloud passes
me by on his way
to the mountains

how does it
feel to wake up
at night
beneath a table in
anyone's dream?

all day long
the waddle of
pregnant girls

Jack FruitMoon

she makes love
when the moon isn't
looking
in a tricycle cab
for the usual fare

heavy rain
pregnant girls bobbing
in flood water

vendors sell
themselves at a
discount to
the men who turn
off their electricity

a spider
doing push-ups
on sticky rice

your smile
wriggles like an eel
struggling to
free itself from the
fisherman's net

humid night . . .
her address on a crumpled
piece of paper

at dawn,
your scent in beads
upon my
chest; the cry of a
vendor selling eggs

new year's eve . . .
old men in the patio
sucking shrimp heads

Jack FruitMoon

croon to me,
moon, with a soft voice . . .
a chorus
of light singing stars
into existence

starlit sky . . .
the river
lined with lanterns

my brother
in-law drinks gin tonight
with the moon
in the back room
of a titty bar

above me,
a rat accepting
darkness

i step out
of your mind like
a two month
old baby, one
step at a time

the morning
painted with a
rooster's sadness

teach me,
lizard, how to
banish
hunger in a
moment's notice

monsoon wind . . .
parting ulam
with a red fork

Jack FruitMoon

the rice field . . .
watching a heron
stretch her wings

i close my
ears to chase the
moon like a
dog playing with
rubber squeak toys

perhaps i
wasn't meant to sleep . . .
ah rain!

Friday night . . .
christmas lights and
the scent
of males who
haven't showered . . .

a light mist
and the mother who
will follow

a small mound
of dirt, the stillness
of words
caught between a
siren's echo

do the
worms know?
storm clouds!

bubbles
each one a dream
leaving me
midway between
scenes in a movie

Jack FruitMoon

a frog, i'd
be careful entering
water

chastening
the sun, a charcoal
vendor
breathing what's left
of yesterday

listen,
butterfly, to
the wind

in her
reflection, she's
bigger
than the snail
eating their labor

if i hugged you
tree, would you
stop shaking?

over tea
my father told
me that
haiku was more than
a three-lined poem

the pakwan
vendor staring at
storm clouds

on our street
the ice cream man
sells youth
to bald-headed men
who can't afford cars

Jack FruitM oon

a widower
talking to the
calamansi tree

after the
third bell, the wind
takes her
place among the trees . . .
a mother to orphans

the smoke
of a bad dream . . .
and fish heads

every time
she cuts a fish head
the turning
of ghosts, the breath
of a dragon

make the most
of it, fly . . .
autumn shortens

Glossary of Tagalog (Filipino) words and terms:

ampalaya: bitter gourd used in Philippine dishes

balut: a a cook egg with a half formed chicken inside

Bataan: city in the Philippines

Bulacan: a province and provincial capital on the island of Luzon in the Philippines

bayawak: monitor lizard

buko juice: fresh coconut milk

carabao: water buffalo

crablets: tiny crabs

durian: a small juicy fruit with a foul smell

halo halo: a dessert made from fruit, beans, crushed ice, milk, leche flan, and soy beans

Jack Fruit: a huge, funny looking fruit that looks like a cross between a melon and a toad's back.

Jeepney: Indigenous to the Philippines, it is a colorful vehicle originally made from WWII jeep parts used for public transportation

lugaw: a form of porridge

lolo: an old man

MacArthur Highway: a crowded highway in Manila and Bulacan

Jack FruitMoon

naga: a hardwood tree

opo: yes sir, yes madame

pakwan: watermelon

palengke: outdoor wet market

pancit: a filipino dish resembling chow mein

patis: a sauce(topping)made from sardines and water

Peso: Filipino dollar

rambutan: a juicy red fruit related to the lechee

sampaguita ilang ilang: the Philippine national flower, It is white
and often sold by street people.

sinigang: a soup

taho: a dessert made from soy bean curd

tilapia: a fresh water fish

Tricycle: a motorbike with an attached cab

ulam: a food dish bought from food vendors

videoke: a bar with prostitutes

About the Author

Robert D. Wilson lives in the Republic of the Philippines with his wife, Jinky. He's a retired educator, newspaper staff writer, magazine columnist, and Southern Baptist minister. Wilson's the co-founder and owner/managing editor of *Simply Haiku*. For years Wilson served as the master of ceremonies for monthly open mike poetry readings in Sonora, California. He's performed his poetry on radio, television, and in a variety of public venues. Wilson's poetry and haiga have been widely published throughout the English speaking world. His haiku and tanka have been translated in the Japanese, Romanian, Serbian, Italian, French, and Tagalog languages. Robert D. Wilson is the father of six children. Not bad for a 59 year old, hard to figure out, and definitely unpredictable "kano."

Also from MODERN ENGLISH TANKA PRESS

Meals at Midnight ⁀ Poems by
Michael McClintock

Lilacs After Winter ⁀ Francis Masat

Proposing to the Woman in the Rear
View Mirror ⁀ Haiku & Senryu by
James Tipton.

Abacus: Prose poems, haibun & short
poems ⁀ Gary LeBel

Looking for a Prince: a collection of
senryu and kyoka ⁀ Alexis Rotella

The Tanka Prose Anthology ⁀
Jeffrey Woodward, Ed.

Greetings from Luna Park ⁀ Sedoka,
James Roderick Burns

In Two Minds ⁀ Responsive Tanka
by Amelia Fielden and Kathy Kituai

An Unknown Road ⁀ Haiku by
Adelaide B. Shaw

Slow Motion: The Log of a
Chesapeake Skipjack ⁀ M. Kei

Ash Moon Anthology: Poems on
Aging in Modern English Tanka ⁀
Alexis Rotella & Denis M. Garrison,
Eds.

Fire Blossoms: The Birth of Haiku
Noir ⁀ Denis M. Garrison

Cigarette Butts and Lilacs: tokens of a
heritage ⁀ Tanka by Andrew Riutta

Sailor in the Rain and Other Poems ⁀
Denis M. Garrison

Four Decades on My Tanka Road:
Tanka Collections of Sanford
Goldstein ⁀ Sanford Goldstein. Fran
Witham, Ed.

this hunger, tissue-thin: new & sel.
tanka 1995–2005 ⁀ Larry Kimmel

Jun Fujita, Tanka Pioneer ⁀ Denis
M. Garrison, Ed.

Landfall: Poetry of Place in Mod. Eng.
Tanka ⁀ Denis M. Garrison and
Michael McClintock, Eds.

Lip Prints: Tanka and Other Short
Poems 1979-2007 ⁀ Alexis Rotella

Ouch: Senryu That Bite ⁀ Alexis
Rotella

Eavesdropping: Seasonal Haiku ⁀
Alexis Rotella

Tanka Teachers Guide ⁀ Denis M.
Garrison, Ed.

Five Lines Down: A Landmark in
English Tanka ⁀ Denis M. Garrison,
Ed.

Sixty Sunflowers: TSA Members'
Anthology 2006-2007 ⁀ Sanford
Goldstein, Ed.

The Dreaming Room: Mod. Eng.
Tanka in Collage and Montage Sets ⁀
Michael McClintock and Denis M.
Garrison, Eds.

Haiku Harvest 2000-2006 ⁀ Denis
M. Garrison, Ed.

Eight Shades of Blue ⁀ Haiku by
Denis M. Garrison

The Salesman's Shoes ⁀ Tanka,
James Roderick Burns

Hidden River ⁀ Haiku by Denis M.
Garrison

The Five-Hole Flute: Modern English
Tanka in Sequences and Sets ⁀ Denis
M. Garrison and Michael McClintock,
Eds.

Journals

⁀ Modern English Tanka ⁀
⁀ Atlas Poetica ⁀
⁀ Modern Haiga ⁀
⁀ Ambrosia ⁀ Prune Juice ⁀
⁀ Modern Haibun & Tanka Prose ⁀